The Engaged Woman's

PRAYER BOOK

SELINA ALMODOVAR

The Engaged Woman's Prayer Book
Copyright © 2019 Selina Almodovar, LLC.
All rights reserved.

No part of this book may be used or reproduced by any means, graphic, electronic, or mechanical, including photocopying, recording, taping or by any information storage retrieval system without the written permission of the publisher.

Copying this book is both illegal and unethical.

Readers should be aware that Internet websites listed in this work may have been changed or disappeared between when this work was written and when it was is read.

Scripture verses marked in NKJV are taken from the New King James Version of the Bible.
Scripture verses marked in NIV are taken from the New International Version of the Bible.
Scripture verses marked in NLT are taken from the New Living Translation Version of the Bible.
Scripture verses marked in MSG are taken from The Message Version of the Bible.
Scripture verses marked in ESV are taken from the English Standard Version of the Bible.

Book Cover Design: Katie Bailey
Book Formatting: Dallas Hodge, www.ebeetbee.com
Editing: Dallas Hodge, www.ebeetbee.com
Author Photo: Ellen Stephens

Dedication

To my husband, Kyle. We're doing it! And I couldn't do ANY of it without you! Thank you. I will forever love you.

To Anita. You inspired Kyle and I to plant our marriage foundation firmly in the love of Christ. I thank you for showing me how to set up a marriage covered in prayer, and for continuing to pray for us and our future. Thank you for encouraging me to pray during my season of engagement. I pray that your influence in me will now influence countless brides-to-be around the world. I love you to the moon and back. Thank you.

Contents

Dedication i

About this Book 1

"What Makes You Know I'm the One" 1

Why You Need Prayer Now More Than Ever ... 9

Why A Prayer Book for Engaged Women? 14

For the Seasoned Prayer Warriors 16

How to Use This Book 18

Self Prayers 21

Wedding Prayers 22

Preparing for Marriage Prayers 22

Bonus Prayers 23

A Few Other Things 24

Scriptures 24

Personal Prayers 24

Answered Prayers 25

Vision Casting with God 26

Self Prayers 29

Prayer of Salvation 30

Making the Right Choice 35

Peace to Move Forward 40

Staying Pure Throughout
the Engagement.. 45
Loving Myself & My Body Image 51
Breaking Past Bondage 57
Removing Stress, Anxiety, Frustration;
Receiving Peace of Mind 63
God Will Provide Counsel & Counselors 69
Strengthen My Relationship with God
As I Strengthen My Relationship
with My Fiancé 75
Saying "Goodbye" To My Single Life 81

Wedding Prayers 87
The Wedding Ceremony Prayer.................... 88
The Wedding Reception Prayer 93
Stress-Free Wedding Prep Season 99
Wedding Be Aligned with God's Vision 105
Wedding Traditions That Would
Align With (Y)Our Values............................. 111
Prayer for the Bridal Party............................ 117
The Wedding Day Prayer 123
The Wedding Night Prayer 129
The Honeymoon Prayer............................... 136

Preparing For Marriage Prayers 142
Prayer for My Future Husband..................... 143
Building a Firm Marriage Foundation......... 149
Prayer For The Blending Of Our Families .. 155
Submitting to My Future Husband............. 162
Dismissing "Divorce" From My Marriage ... 168

Prayer Over Our Joint Finances 174
Prep Me For a New Season As a Wife 180
Becoming One Body 186
Effective Communication With
My Future Husband 192

Bonuses! 198

Bonus Prayers! 202
Prayer for My Children During My
Engagement Session 203
Preparing for the New
Role as a Step-Mom 210
Prayer For My Second (or Third) Marriage 217
If The Engagement Breaks Off 223
How To Pray With Your Fiancé 229
How To Cast Vision with God 235
Tips for a Smooth Engagement Session 237

Now What? 241
Acknowledgments 246

About this Book

"What Makes You Know I'm the One?"

I woke up that Thursday morning with the warm sun shining in my face, so I decided to wear one of my favorite dresses. You ever wake up to one of those days where you just know that it's gonna be a good day? My work schedule consisted of a bunch of meetings with some really good people that would have me in and out of my office all day, and my night was ending with a small group that I attended with some of my closest friends, including my boyfriend, Kyle.

Yup, it was going to be a good day and I declared it before even rolling out of bed.

I remember how perfectly my lunch hour coincided with Kyle's that day, which almost never happened in the spring since he drove around the city a lot for his job. Yet, as He does, God brought us together to enjoy a short, yet lovely lunch.

We chatted about nothing and were very much in love. In the end, we planned to get together before heading to our life group. I suggested going to our favorite park–the one where we developed a friendship as youth group leaders. The same one where we decided to start dating and confessed our love for one another. It was our park. And I couldn't wait.

My afternoon carried on and it went by pretty fast. I remember staying at my office just a tad bit too late to stop home to change out of my dress before our "mini-date". My business-casual attire would have to do for that evening.

I met Kyle in the parking lot and together we walked to the edge of the park, near the lake. We went to our favorite little place on the "do not step on the rocks" rocks where the lake splashed softly against the slabs of rock, while the city skyline stood tall in front of us. It was picture-perfect.

There were a few teenage girls sitting nearby on our left while a couple of young boys gathered to our right. Several photographers stood nearby with their cameras capturing the beauty that the day displayed. Life was all around us, enhancing the beauty of the day.

And much like our lunch conversation, we chatted about nothing and soaked up every minute of it. At some point, we began to talk about certainty. As in, how could I know that I would love Kyle forever? Naturally, I began to think out loud and count all of the ways that I knew I could love him.

You see, by this time, after dating each other for a little under a year, I grew to love my friend with a very pure passion. Having never kissed him before, I grew confident in knowing that the love I felt for Kyle was real and genuine. And through it all, I had prayed and fasted to God for Kyle, and eventually with Kyle, about our love for each other and the future of our relationship.

There was no doubt left in me. I wanted very much to become his wife. It wasn't a sudden thought or consideration. My feelings for him were a sure thing.

After concluding my answer to Kyle, he helped me up from the rock we had been sitting on to prepare to leave the park and head to small group together. As he was lifting me up, I shot the question back at him.

"What makes YOU know I'm the One?"

He naturally smiled. He stared in my eyes while brushing my hair back and behind my ears. He chuckled briefly and held my arms, taking in the moment and all that it was.

I, on the other hand, was dead serious! After all the loving things I had just gushed out, he had better come up with something good! I mean, don't get me wrong. I already knew the answer–we talked about this all before. We attended marriage retreats, seminars, classes, studied books, listened to sermon series on marriage, love, and relationships, and we prayed. Hard.

We both knew how we felt towards each other. But it was still nice to hear it every now and then. So as I anxiously awaited to hear his reason for loving me for the hundredth time, he slowly moved his hands from my arms to holding my hands. Then he said...

"Selina, there is no doubt in my mind that I will love you forever..."

And just like that, he dropped to one knee and continued with, "Will you marry me?"

Out of nowhere. Just like that. Time stood still. Everything stopped. Just like in the movies. Exactly like in the movies!

I looked down and sure enough, there was a tiny white box in his hands, with a shiny diamond ring.

With the gorgeous Thursday sun shining down on it, the lake softly cooed behind us, reminding me that the world was still spinning. All while trying to stop my own world from spinning. Was this seriously happening?!

I suddenly looked to my left to see the teenage girls staring back at me, jaws dropped, earbuds officially out of their ears. I noticed a lone photographer aiming his camera squarely in our direction. And then I looked back down at Kyle.

Yup, he was still there. And so was that ring. And I was totally freaking out.

I cupped my hands over my mouth and for the first time in a really long time, I was speechless. But the voice inside my head was going a mile a minute. So to stall, in order to process what the heck was happening in that year-in-the-making moment, I answered Kyle by saying,

"Um, what are you doing?"

I think I may have asked him that about twenty times, which gave me enough time to think of the following:

"How could he have planned this when I was the one who suggested going to the park only hours ago??"

"That's not the ring I kept showing him...."

"Is this really happening?"

"After all these years, all those guys... all that pain... is this how it really happens?"

"Do I really deserve this?"

"Am I even ready to be his wife?"

"What if I mess up?"

"What if I tell him that I gotta think about it for a few days?"

"This is the moment I've been waiting for! Why am I doubting now?"

"Am I really ready for my entire life to change from this moment on?"

"It already has."

"This is really happening."
"Trust God."
"Say yes!"

Even now, as I write this, being happily married now for going on six years, I weep at the reminder of how much God loves me that He would give me such a gift and blessing on that beautiful day–a proposal to become Kyle's wife!

When I finally said "yes" (after what seemed like a straight 20 minutes!) Kyle stood up and cheered. The girls to our left clapped. The photographer crept his way closer and closer to us. Kyle slipped off my purity ring from my left ring finger and moved it to my right hand. Then he slowly slipped on my new engagement ring.

He hugged me deeply and continued to lift his hands in the air in a victory pose. All those thoughts I had only moments before suddenly vanished. The tears began to trickle down. I still could not believe it was all happening. I was overwhelmed with happiness.

I felt like I had just defeated some great big monster that used to haunt my love-life.

Finally, no more breakups! No more feelings of being used or cheated on. I would never again feel those feelings. I knew that Kyle would live out the rest of his days loving me in a way that God showed him how to love.

After our initial celebration, I discovered that the photographer was a friend of ours, and was asked to be there by Kyle. It was all real–and now we would have the pictures to prove it. This was my life.

It took us a while to make our way back to our cars. I became so overwhelmed that I would cry to the point of hyperventilation, then I had to stop and breathe. Then I couldn't think at all. I tried to think of the simplest of things–what to call the sky, the lake, or even the word for "grass", and I couldn't. My mind literally went blank. That is until I remembered what just happened only moments ago. Cue the waterworks. In came the hyperventilation. Couldn't remember anything. Again.

This went on for almost an hour. Dramatic much? It was the happiest day of my life.

Once that happened, we finally made our way out of the park. We visited all of our parents (his folks and mine, who were divorced) to tell them the good news. Finally, after receiving the blessings of our parents, we celebrated with our friends. I could not have planned it any better.

On the car ride to our parent's house, I tried to share my fears of what lied ahead with Kyle.

"What is something happens and we get a di–"

"No. You are never allowed to say that word. Ever."

That night I cried and prayed harder than I ever had before. My inner being cried out to God from all of the emotions I had felt that day.

No matter how much studying and preparing we did as a couple and as individuals, nothing could have prepared me to feel what I felt on that day.

Thank You, Jesus, I was finally engaged!!!

Why You Need Prayer Now More Than Ever

Going home that night was such a blur. As cliché as this may sound, I could not stop looking at that ring!

After speaking to our parents and our closest friends, it was time to take our news to social media. You know when you announce something on Facebook, it's super official. And we were super official. I just couldn't believe it.

And naturally, everyone wanted to know what comes next.

"So when are you gonna get married?"

"Hmmm… never really thought about it."

I'm lying. I've thought about this since I was five. Since the movie "The Little Mermaid" came out and I fell in love with her wedding. The veil, the pink nails, the royal families of the land and sea coming together under a glorious rainbow.

Yeah… now that I was actually thinking about it, I guess I did need to consider these questions more realistically.

And once you go down that rabbit hole, there is no turning back. So. Many. Things to consider!

Of course, you have the important decision of actually deciding *when* to get married. But then you start thinking about everything else that throws you off completely!

For example, a date cannot be set until you determine the ideal *season* that you'd like to get married in. Kyle proposed to me in the late spring, and well, I always envisioned getting married in the spring, so did that mean we'd have to wait an entire year to get married?

Oh, then there are other important dates that could play a factor (vacations, work stuff, families' birthdays, other people's anniversaries, national holidays, etc.) Wait… what about the people who will get invited, like my grandparents in Puerto Rico? Can they attend a wedding on the day that I was thinking about having it, or does it need to be changed?

Hold up, what about the church and a reception venue? Are those even available on the day that I wanna get married?

Can we even afford this? How much time should we have to save up for this wedding?

Should we just elope and forget the whole thing completely?

Yes.

No! Geesh, what would my grandma think?

So. Many. Things to consider.

And while this conversation actually happened to me multiple times throughout my engagement, I can guess that you probably had a good chuckle when you read it because you felt the same way.

So many questions. Not enough answers. And while you're soaring on cloud nine from this amazing thing that just happened to you, if you're aren't careful, the overwhelming thoughts of it all could take over completely and leave you feeling lost, stressed, frustrated, and very anxious.

Sister, this is why you need prayer now more than ever!

First of all, your engagement was a God thing. Amen! Or... was it? Only through prayer will you know for sure.

Sure, for the most part, we all tend to focus on the "big day". But rest assured, that day only lasts 24 hours, whereas the vows you take on that special day will commit you to many, many, many more.

An engagement is a time where you prepare your life to become something new. It is a time where God is creating a new thing. A new marriage. A new union of two souls. A new covenant between God and two hearts. A new family out of two, very unique families. All of which is gonna require some serious prayer in order to stay close to God and His will over your life and this new season.

And while you may be the perfect girlfriend, becoming a wife is a totally different ballgame.

Praying throughout this season, for yourself, your wedding day, and your marriage is the key to setting a firm foundation required for a successful marriage.

Not to worry! You will be ready in due time! It's a process. Something that will require great amounts of time, patience, growth, and trust in God. These are all the benefits you receive from... you guessed it. Prayer.

Just as a woman becomes pregnant, she isn't prepared to be a mother to that child the very next day. Nor is the child prepared to meet its mommy. There's a process. A season of growth. And in that season, both the mother and the child change in preparation for the birth and life thereafter.

So, as you're replaying your proposal over and over in your head, I want you to enjoy it.

As you cannot get enough of the ring that now sits perfectly on your ring finger, your new most favorite ring in the whole wide world, I want you to enjoy it.

Embrace that glow that you are now wearing–it looks perfect on you.

And if you find yourself feeling a bit... off... worry not.

The questions will come. The overwhelming will try to sneak its way in. Stress will be banging at your door. Conflicts will arise. And everyone will have something to say about it all.

Prayer will get you through this season.

Prayer will help you embrace the good and deal with the bad.

Prayer will remind you that God is for you and never against you.

Prayer will make this one of the most beautiful, wonderful, effortless, and glorious seasons of your life.

Can I get an "Amen"?

Why A Prayer Book for Engaged Women?

When I wrote my first book, "The Single Woman's Prayer Book" in 2017, I always knew that it would become a part of a series. And I always knew that the next installment of that series would be catered to engaged women.

Much like the problem I had in my single days, I frankly could not find a prayer book that was specific to the needs of those who are engaged.

Sure, there are countless resources on how to prepare for marriage. And many more that focus on what you should do to prepare for the wedding day. But nothing was really out there for a woman who was going through it all and in need of prayers that could help her present God with these situations.

Not to mention, this was a crucial time in my own life where I was beginning to sew my life with my future husband's. There were many things that came up during our premarital counseling that I never really thought about that led me to pray some personal prayers not often found in the prayer books at the time.

As I'm sure you may have also discovered during this time, weddings are a billion-dollar industry. The pressures of having the perfect dress for the perfect wedding can become super stressful. Of course, if you have the perfect dress then you gotta have the perfect body, which then leads to dieting, weight loss obsessions, and pressure to "look" a certain way.

Can I just add that the financial pressures to make this all possible is a topic all on its own!

And this is just the beginning. We haven't even talked about two becoming one. One home. One family. One future. Maybe it's just me talking here, but I want it ALL covered in prayer!

So while finding the joy and contentment in being single is one (very important) season to have deep roots of prayer in, preparing to become a wife is just as important.

Why not cover every inch of it in prayer?

You may or may not have set a firm foundation at the beginning stages of your relationship with your fiancé centered in Christ. Whether you did or are just beginning to think about it, I think your engagement season is the perfect time to solidify that faith and trust in God for your future.

For the Seasoned Prayer Warriors

As I mentioned above, coming to a place of engagement is a beautiful blessing. And if you've been close to God throughout this entire process (being single, meeting your Mr. Right, and developing a relationship with him) then you are probably pretty sure that getting engaged was a total God move. Amen!

But now is when things start to get a bit tricky. God loves marriage. He loves family. He designed it before sin ever came into the picture! And the enemy knows how powerful a married couple under the hand of God can be.

So, the enemy will try to keep you from seeing this through at all costs! Remember, the enemy is petty! He is here "walking about like a roaring lion, seeking whom he may devour." (1 Peter 5:8). Because of that, we are called to be sober and vigilant! We must carefully watch for any possible danger or difficulties that come our way!

If you are a seasoned prayer warrior and you decided to pick up this book then I'm praying that my prayers combined with your own personal prayers will together create an amazing covering over you, your fiancé, your wedding, and your future marriage. Use the topics that I provide in this book to help address details and concerns that perhaps you may have overlooked.

And know that I am coming into agreement with any and all prayers that you are lifting up on your own throughout this season as well!

While many of these prayers were the same prayers I've prayed during my engagement experience, I hope that they will also shed some light and truth to your heart's concerns, needs, and desires. Not to mention breakthroughs that you are in line to receive during this season of your life.

Getting engaged is all about preparing for a new thing in your life. And as a seasoned prayer warrior knows, preparation is the very essence of prayer! It is in the time of prayer that you will be able to fully prepare your heart, mind, body, and spirit for what God has in store for you. May this book be a tool, a resource, and a gift of support from me to you. And may it continue to keep you close to God and His will over your love life.

How to Use This Book

This book was created with the assumption that you already have a grasp of what prayer is and how it works. If you have never prayed before in your life, and this is totally a new thing for you, then allow me to break it down for you.

Prayer is our way of communicating with God. (Lamentations 3:41)

Prayer is a conversation. (Jeremiah 29: 12-13)

We speak to God through prayer, and in His time, God will speak back to us.

Prayer is very personal and intimate. (Matthew 6:6)

Because God already knows our hearts, we are basically using this time to express our love for God by spending time with Him and opening up ourselves to Him. Think of a child with their parent. The parent is fully aware that something is going on with their child, but more than anything, that parent just wants their child to come to them to talk and be open with them. It is a moment of adoration and love. And that is what God is seeking in this time with you!

Prayer is a time to get real with yourself. (Psalm 145:18)

To come clean about your thoughts, your struggles, and your feelings.

Prayer is a time to seek God in the way that you most need Him (counsel, wisdom, discernment, comfort, peace, etc.) (Matthew 21:22)

Prayer is to come correct your wrongs and seek forgiveness from God for those wrongs. (Mark 11:25)

While prayer is so much more than this, which you can learn about by using other resources, this book is geared to help you reach each of these points through the use of my personal prayers.

Prayer books are what helped me develop my own prayer voice. While I initially began using prayer books simply because I did not have the right words to say at the time of my praying, over time, I was able to feel comfortable enough to know what to pray for, how to incorporate scriptures into my prayers and develop a desire to pray often.

This prayer book is geared towards what you would most likely pray for during your engagement season. Whether you purchased this book on your own, or you received it as a gift, using this book throughout your time as an engaged woman will produce many benefits as you move towards your wedding day and marriage.

Regardless of how long this particular season is, you can use these prayers over and over until you receive answers for those specific prayers, or just until your season ends.

I wanted to make this book as simple as possible for you. While I recommend going through each category in the order that it was written, you can most certainly go to any prayer you want (or need) without feeling like you are out of sequence.

If you need a quick prayer regarding something specific because you're feeling a certain way, then go for it. However, if you are simply looking to use this prayer book as a guided daily devotional, then the beginning of this book will be your best starting point.

There are a total of 27 prayers in this book. They are divided into four categories:

Self Prayers

While everything that comes with a wedding is nice, all eyes will be on the bride. So not only do you have to prepare yourself to look your best, but you also need to feel your best! You should feel absolute peace when you wake up on your wedding day and as you carry on into your marriage.

The prayers contained in this section will allow you to produce just that. They are meant to help you find peace in your heart and spirit to move forward as the bride, and as a future wife. So all those bridezillas out there that we see, yeah, that's not gonna be you! Why? Because you are gonna be praying over this season to have peace through and through.

This section is also meant to bring you peace about how you feel when it comes to yourself and how you appear on the outside. Making sure that you feel beautiful and are mindful of your health and self-care (which can definitely fly out the window if you aren't careful!)

Lastly, these prayers are meant for you to maintain the relationship that you have with Christ as a woman of God. While it is true that "two will become one", it is still very important that you maintain your personal relationship with God and not place anything or anyone in place of it.

Wedding Prayers

These prayers will cover the actual day (and night) of your wedding. Have you ever heard the horror stories of something going terribly wrong on the day of the wedding? Yeah, also not going to be you! Believe me when I say that it is truly possible to have an "effortless" wedding day and an unforgettable wedding night. But prayer plays a major role in making that possible.

So, as many overwhelming details as there are when it comes to planning out your special day, these prayers are meant to cover every last one of them.

Preparing for Marriage Prayers

If you think that planning the wedding was a lot, it doesn't even come close to the lifelong adventure that is to come the day after.

This section is meant to help cover you, your future husband, and your marriage covenant so that you are blessed and highly favored from day one. There are many reasons why people end their marriages–these prayers are designed to cover many of those attacks!

Bonus Prayers

In this day and age, it is very common to have second marriages or blended families. While this is not the case for everyone, this section does, in fact, offer specific prayers for those specific cases!

This section will also have a few extra resources to help you plan out your wedding day, tips on praying with your fiancé, and special wedding ceremony and reception prayers that you can use!

The free handouts mentioned in this section are also available for you online at:

http://selinaalmodovar.com/EWPBResources

A Few Other Things

Scriptures

There are a few Scriptures that came to mind as I prayed these prayers. Use these as references, verses to meditate on, or as a way to dig deeper into the Word that can be paired with your prayers.

Throughout this book, I have often used the New King James Version (NKJV) because it is my favorite. However, please feel free to reference these verses using your favorite Bible version!

Personal Prayers

I want you to use this space to jot down any additional prayer points you may have that I've left out. Really own these prayers. God already knows your heart, so there's nothing really to hide from Him. Writing out your prayers will be like putting all of your cards on the table. You're pretty much exposing all that you have going on in this particular area. When you choose to do that, you are choosing to trust God with it, and you surrender your control over it, which are both really, really good things. So, I encourage you to stretch yourself and utilize this space. Because prayer works. And your personal prayers will work too if you feed them your faith.

You can read through this book in its entirety while jotting down your own personal prayers. Once you've finished, you can go through this book again and come out with a totally new experience because now you have those added prayers! If you need a few pointers on how to create your own personal prayer, you can check out the "Creating Your Own Prayer" handout at:

http://selinaalmodovar.com/EWPBResources

Answered Prayers

It is always extremely awesome and rewarding to go back and see how far you've come. It's important to recognize when God has moved in your life because it will increase your faith, increase your hope, and encourage you to keep going!

So use this section to address any answers you've received from a specific prayer!

Vision Casting with God

Unlike my first book, "The Single Woman's Prayer Book", I've decided to include this new section specifically to help you and your Fiancé include God in the planning and preparations of your wedding and marriage.

If you're not quite sure what this means, it's simply put; these are the notes you take when you have your meetings with God.

Picture it like going to meet with your personal wedding planner. You sit with them and you begin to discuss your vision for your wedding day. What you want, what you like, and what you can afford, all that jazz. Together, with your planner, you come up with all the steps to execute your vision in the best way possible.

Much like how this can totally happen with your wedding planner, you will practice doing this with God. And because He will always have your best interest at heart, it's very important that you seek Him first above anyone else!

Through prayer, whenever the Lord reveals His desires for our hearts, He will cast a vision so that you can put it into action for the glory of God.

"There are many plans in a man's heart, Nevertheless the LORD's counsel–that will stand." – Proverbs 19:21

Kyle and I approached God together for many things when it came to planning our wedding and marriage. Everything down to the budget, who to work with, and how to bless others who helped us throughout our season, was addressed and revealed to us during our vision casting with God.

When it was time to put together our wedding ceremony, the Scriptures and quotes we used, the activities we did during the ceremony, and the order of the ceremony was all revealed to us as we lifted it up in prayer.

And our finances for everything (the dress, the venues, the honeymoon, finding a new house we would both be living in, etc.), which started out as a big stressor, came in increments. We didn't have the entire budget upfront. But as you may know by now, many parts of the wedding and new home require some large upfront fees.

I cannot stress to you how much relying on God during those financial prayer times helped us not only create the right budget, but to also spend what God wanted us to spend *when* He wanted us to spend it.

This is a time when you are planning one of the biggest changes of your life! Trust me when I say, that when you include God in the planning stages, He will most certainly help bring you to your ideal end result!

Check out "How to Cast Vision with God" in the Bonus chapter of this book!

Self Prayers

Prayer of Salvation

Dear Lord,

Creator of all things, heaven, and earth…

I know that You have also created me. Now I am beginning to understand that You also love me more than anything in this world, because I am one of your most precious daughters.

You love me so much that You send Your beloved Son, Jesus Christ, to die for my sins.

I know that if I don't choose You and Your love, my sins will eventually lead me to death. Lord, I humbly ask that You forgive me of those sins.

I ask that You forgive me for _______________, as well as those sins that I've forgotten.

I choose life with You, Lord. I ask You to come into my heart and fill it with Your unending love. Repair my heart, Lord, in a way that only You can.

I want to embrace Your love and everlasting life for the rest of my life. I thank You, Lord, for Your love and for increasing my faith to know You better.

Thank You, Jesus, for dying on the cross for my sins, and for rising up again for me. Thank You for Your unfailing, relentless love. And I thank You for giving me a new life!

Amen.

Scriptures

If you declare with your mouth, "Jesus is Lord," and believe in your heart that God raised Him from the dead, you will be saved. For it is with your heart that you believe and are justified, and it is with your mouth that you profess your faith and are saved.

Romans 10:9-10 (NKJV)

Personal Prayers

Answered Prayers

Vision Casting With God

Making the Right Choice

Dear Lord,

I thank you so much for bringing *(name of fiancé)* into my life. He is more than I could ever imagine in a man. Thank you for allowing me to experience love at this level in my life.

Lord, as we prepare to take this relationship to the next level, I wanna bring You into the equation. I don't want to move towards marriage if it is not a part of Your plan. Lord, I do not want to live a life that is ordained solely by my emotions. Help me to see what You see, despite how I feel. It this is Your will, then reveal it to me in such a way that I know without a doubt that the confirmation is coming straight from You and no one else.

Let me feel a peace about this unlike any other. I trust You, Lord. And as much as I want this to work out and to happen in my life in this season, I definitely don't want to go through it all only for it to end up not being the real thing. I want the real thing. I want what You have for me. The very best.

If this is it, and if *(name of fiancé)* is Your perfect gift for me, then I ask for your Holy Spirit prompting to let it be known.

I thank You, Lord, for Your wisdom, discernment, and guidance over me. For always looking out for me and for always having my best interest at heart.

Amen.

Scriptures

We can make our plans, but the LORD determines our steps.

Proverbs 16:9 (NLT)

Personal Prayers

Answered Prayers

Vision Casting With God

Peace to Move Forward

Dear Lord,

I know that marriage is a big move. And You've brought me so close to it that I feel like I might just burst with sheer excitement. However, there's a part of me that is afraid of the next stage in life.

Everything is moving so fast. And even though I've wanted this for so long, and have prayed over it for a very long time, I feel like I'm about to give up the only life I know for a new life that I know nothing about.

Lord, I know that marriage is of Your creation, so it is a good thing. This fear that I'm feeling, on the other hand, is not. Help me, Lord, to cast out all fear that I have when it comes to moving forward in this new chapter of my life. Remove any fear that I have in walking out on the waters that You have called me to. Give me the courage to say "yes" and to start a fresh chapter in my life as a wife.

Help me to see my faith in this answered prayer. May it be used to build me up and prepare me fully and deeply to become all that You have created me to be.

Amen.

Scriptures

Do not be afraid or discouraged, for the LORD will personally go ahead of you. He will be with you; he will neither fail you nor abandon you.

Deuteronomy 31:8 (NLT)

Personal Prayers

Answered Prayers

Vision Casting With God

Staying Pure Throughout The Engagement Session

Dear Lord,

I thank you for the relationship I have with *(name of fiancé)*. Though I have prayed daily to remain pure in our actions, thoughts, and hearts with each other, I feel like ever since we got engaged, the temptations have gotten worse.

Lord, we are so close to the finish line that I can taste it. Help me to stay pure, especially in these final days as an unmarried woman. Help us, Lord, to cast out any and all temptations of giving ourselves to each other before marriage. Lord, clear my mind and heart of any impurities that would make me want to entertain the thought of going against your plan and commandments.

I pray that You will help us to remain pure in our engagement season. Give us strength in our spirit to overcome our fleshly desires. Help me to remain modest in how I dress and be cautious in what I say or do with *(name of fiancé)*.

Give us a crystal clear way out if any temptation arises.

Help me to continue to discover the heart of this man as I allow him to continue discovering mine. May we be able to fully respect one another, dismiss our own selfishness, pride, or independence, and seek humility from You. Purify us from the inside out.

Amen.

Scriptures

Flee from sexual immorality. Every sin that a man does is outside of the body, but he who commits sexual immorality sins against his own body. Or do you not know that your body is a temple of the Holy Spirit who is in you, whom you have from God, and you are not your own?

1 Corinthians 6:18-19 (NKJV)

Personal Prayers

Answered Prayers

Vision Casting With God

Loving Myself & My Body Image

Dear Lord,

I thank You for bringing me a man who finds me beautiful enough to marry. As beautiful as he makes me feel, I want to feel it for myself.

I pray to maintain a healthy lifestyle and positive image throughout my engagement season. May the dress I find flatter every curve, bone, muscle, and physical trait that You have given me, without the need to lose or gain drastic weight or change the natural beauty that I was born with.

Lord, I pray that I would not allow the pressures of weight or body image affect the blessings that You have given me throughout this season. I pray that You would renew my mind daily so that I would not harbor such negative thoughts.

Remind me that I am a beautiful creation of the Most High; fearfully and wonderfully made in Your glorious image. And Your truths will be more than enough to live confidently in my own skin.

Lord, I ask that if my heart is telling me to live a healthier lifestyle, that the Holy Spirit would lead me to choices that would only empower my beauty, not condemn it. Remove any laziness, excuse-making thoughts, or setbacks that would cause me to not make healthier lifestyle choices.

Through it all, Lord, I pray to feel beautiful from the inside out. May your truth, my fiancé's affirmations, and my own confidence bring out the very best in me this season, and those to come. I give You the glory. And I thank You for guiding me with Your loving truths.

Amen.

Scriptures

Oh yes, you shaped me first inside, then out; you formed me in my mother's womb. I thank you, High God - you're breathtaking! Body and soul, I am marvelously made! I worship in adoration - what a creation! You know me inside and out, you know every bone in my body; You know exactly how I was made, bit by bit, how I was sculpted from nothing into something.

Psalm 139:13-15 (MSG)

Personal Prayers

Answered Prayers

Vision Casting With God

Breaking Past Bondage

Dear Lord,

I've waited for this season for a while. And I thank You for allowing me to enter into it at last. The last thing I want to do is move forward without a clean heart and steadfast spirit.

Lord, I pray that You would reveal to me in this season any unwanted or unnecessary baggage that I am holding onto. Whether it is unintentional or intentional, reveal it to me, and give me the courage and boldness to get rid of it once and for all.

As I prepare for marriage during this season, I want to be sure that my marriage is complete and secure in Your love and Your divine protection. Release any ounce of baggage that I may be holding onto, in the name of Jesus.

I pray that Your Holy Spirit would help me release what and who I am still holding onto in order to have a firm marriage foundation moving forward. Furthermore, I pray that once You reveal this to me that You would give me the spirit of wisdom and discernment as to how I can let this go without bringing up drama, conflict, or strife between my fiancé and I.

Help me to share this with my fiancé so that we can grow stronger as one body and that our foundation would remain strong.

Bring strong women and mentors in my life who can help me take hold of the very thing that has been holding me back for so long. May your power and might take over and free me from these things. More specifically, as I pray this prayer, I want to speak again the following bondages:

____

In the name of Jesus, by the faith that I possess within my heart, I pray that You would remove and banish this bondage over my life for good. I declare freedom, power, and might in Your holy name.

Amen.

Scriptures

This means that anyone who belongs to Christ has become a new person. The old life is gone; a new life has begun!

2 Corinthians 5:17 (NLT)

Personal Prayers

Answered Prayers

Vision Casting With God

Removing Stress, Anxiety, Frustration; Receiving Peace of Mind

Dear Lord,

This is supposed to be one of the happiest seasons of my life. Yet, I cannot honestly feel this wholeheartedly because I feel weighed down by stress. It's causing great anxiety over my mind and heart and I'm disappointed that so much of my thoughts and energy are going into this when it should be going into You, my fiancé, and preparing for the next season of my life.

Lord, where you are, these feelings should not be. I pray that You would take away any frustration, stress, and/or anxiety that I am currently facing because of ___________.

I pray over these people who are a part of my frustration, anxiety and stress: ____________.

And I pray, in the name of Jesus, that you would not only release these emotions from me but replace them with your supernatural peace and reassurance that we are still moving with you in the lead.

Lord, if I still have to deal with these people throughout my wedding planning and premarital preparations, then I ask that you make a way so that those negative feelings and burdens do not return.

Give me wisdom, Lord, in how to deal with these stressful situations. Send someone who can mediate on my behalf. Or show me what I can do instead to diffuse any tension that is created. Lord, I want to feel your peace–I want to look back at this season and call it blessed because it is.

I do not wish to give the enemy any piece of this season. I declare this to be of Your work. Your season and Your plan. If it is not, please reveal it. But if it is, protect it and cover it with your divine calmness and love.

Amen.

Scriptures

Give all your worries and cares to God, for he cares about you.

1 Peter 5:17 (NLT)

Personal Prayers

Answered Prayers

Vision Casting With God

God Will Provide Counsel & Counselors

Dear Lord,

As I prepare for this new season, I wanna say that I think I'll know what to do when it comes to having a lifelong husband. But deep down, I know that I probably don't.

I need You, Lord. I need your wisdom and Your grace. I need to know how to make this marriage last. I want to follow your examples and be led by You and You alone.

I pray that this season I'm in can and will be used as a time for me to prepare my heart, mind, lifestyle, finances, future, and beliefs for becoming a godly wife. Help me to find the right Bible studies, devotionals, events, classes, or anything else that will offer me and my fiancé the counsel we need to effectively prepare for a life and marriage together.

Also, I pray that you reveal to us the right counselor to help us actively engage in premarital counseling. I don't want someone who will merely go through the motions or waste our time.

Bring us someone who will genuinely care for our future and their part in securing that future. Someone who is fair and easy to talk to and learn from. I pray that they would be used by You, along with any tools and resources You reveal to us so that we can dismiss any fears and doubts that we may have when it comes to preparing for marriage and life as one.

I thank you, Lord, for always taking care of me and having my best interest at heart. I thank you for our counselor and for offering me and my fiancé counsel whenever we need and ask for it. You are our wonderful Counselor. And your wisdom is light to our union.

Amen.

Scriptures

The way of a fool is right in his own eyes, But he who heeds counsel is wise.

Proverbs 12:15 (NKJV)

Personal Prayers

Answered Prayers

Vision Casting With God

Strengthen My Relationship with God As I Strengthen My Relationship with My Fiance

Dear Lord,

My heart and love for my fiancé *(name of fiancé)* are so full that only You can receive the glory for all of my joy and happiness. I pray that the love I have for him will never fade and that we always put You first in our marriage over all else.

However, as much as I love *(name of fiancé)* and want to continue to strengthen our relationship, I pray that I can also establish and stand firm in my relationship with You. Lord, as a single woman, I have cherished many moments with You. And You have molded me into the woman of faith that I am today.

But with so much attention now going into this marriage, I do not want to put you on the back burner. Help me to put You first before any and all things, Lord. Remind me to always include you in my marriage and in my own thoughts and actions as a woman of God.

I pray, Lord, that You will give me faith when I have none, reveal my time that I could be spending with You whenever I intentionally/unintentionally waste it. And help me to never forget to seek You first over everyone else, including *(name of fiancé)*.

Lord, I want my relationship with You to strengthen just as much as my relationship with *(name of fiancé)* is strengthening, if not more.

I pray that while my time with you may look different once I'm married, that I always remember to make time with you no matter what.

Amen.

Scriptures

But as for me, how good it is to be near God! I have made the Sovereign LORD my shelter, and I will tell everyone about the wonderful things you do.

Psalm 73:28 (NLT)

Personal Prayers

Answered Prayers

Vision Casting With God

Saying "Goodbye" To My Single Life

Dear Lord,

As I live out these final days as a "single woman", I just wanna thank you, Lord. I thank You for meeting me where I was all this time and for always being faithful.

Thank You for molding me into the woman I have become and for preparing me to become the wife You have called me to be. Lord, I thank You for revealing Your love to me when I needed it most. Thank You for teaching me how to love myself and to love others. Thank You for using me in this season and stretching me to believe in You more and Your power.

And through it all, You still answered my prayers of finding a man worthy of marrying me! Because even in the times when I doubted, You were faithful and mindful of me.

Thank You for revealing this blessing to me. There is nothing You cannot do! I pray that my season of singleness can be used to glorify You however possible. I pray that my story can help others see and know that You are a good God with our best interests at heart. I pray that You would use me in my next season just as much as You did in my last season.

Thank You, God, for being so awesome and for finally revealing to me why the wait felt so long. I see now that it was all a part of Your perfect plan. I praise You for it.

And I thank You.

Amen.

Scriptures

For of Him and through Him and to Him are all things, to whom be glory forever. Amen.

Romans 11:36 (NKJV)

Personal Prayers

Answered Prayers

Vision Casting With God

Wedding Prayers

The Wedding Ceremony Prayer

Dear Lord,

I pray that You would abundantly bless the bride and groom on their wedding day. May they be full of gladness, and adorned with the jewels of Your love and prosperity. Clothe them in peace and serenity. Unveil Your glory in this place for all to witness and receive.

Bless the hands that were used to make this wedding day all that it is. May every vendor, helper, and contributor receive Your blessings and favor for their service and faith in this couple and their future.

Bless the family and friends who have gathered to witness this day in history. To celebrate the love of the cherished couple and to proclaim the goodness of what their love will accomplish from this day forward. Thank You, Lord, for bringing these souls here today safely, timely, and with the expectation that they will assist and support the vows and covenant that will be made today in Your name.

Lord, may You continuously bless the bride and groom all the days of their lives. Allow increase to overflow in their home, finances, family, health, ministry, friendship, and love for one another.

I thank You, Lord, that You have ordained this day, and all that comes from it, as the day when love wins again. A day that has been marked as a beautiful moment You have personally orchestrated that will reap blessings and new creations for generations to come.

We give You the glory,

Amen.

Scriptures

Therefore what God has joined together, let not man separate.

Mark 10:9 (NKJV)

Personal Prayers

Answered Prayers

Vision Casting With God

The Wedding Reception Prayer

Dear Lord,

We are thankful to be a part of Your blessings and celebrations of the bride and groom today. As we rejoice in their union and sacred marriage, we pray to mark this moment as a beautiful memory that we will always remember for years to come.

Bless the food and those who prepared it. Bless the desserts and other portions of this meal. As we break bread together, may we come together and fellowship happily. May our love for one another reflect the love that we have for the bride and groom.

Bless the hands who served the bride and groom in decorating the place and bringing life into it. Bless the entertainment tonight–may they all be blessed by serving as a blessing to us today.

We pray that there would be no negative outcomes, opinions, actions, or behaviors that would affect this event. May You cover this place with your protection and peace. We are here to have a great time and let nothing or no one keep us from doing so.

We are thankful to be a part of this moment. And we are thankful to be a witness of Your love and goodness. We invite You into every room and corner of this place. Fill it with Your love, joy, peace, patience, kindness, goodness, gentleness, faithfulness, and self-control. We praise Your name for all You have done in this season that led up to this moment.

We give You the glory, God.

Amen.

Scriptures

Therefore, whether you eat or drink, or whatever you do, do all to the glory of God.

1 Corinthians 10:31 (NKJV)

Personal Prayers

Answered Prayers

Vision Casting With God

Stress-Free Wedding Prep Season

Dear Lord,

I lift up this engagement to You and every good thing that comes from it. I praise You, Lord, for allowing us to step into this season. I trust in Your guidance and discernment throughout.

Lord, as we begin to prepare for our wedding, I ask that You make this a smooth and effortless experience. For everything that we are asking for–from the venue to the flowers to the caterer to the dress and honeymoon location, I pray that we would find all of the right vendors to work with who would be able to cast our vision with ease.

I pray for our finances to be in order at this time and that everything we need for our wedding would align with our budget. Whatever seems out of reach, Lord, I pray that You would give us the discernment and wisdom on how to make it work or give us the peace to carry on without it.

Lord, I pray that I do not become a "bridezilla". Help me to cast my vision to those who are willing to help without a spirit of control or anxiety. Help me to adopt Your spirit of love, kindness, and gentleness. But also, Lord, I ask that You put the right people in my corner who are willing to help, step up, and support our vision throughout this season.

I pray, Lord, that my health and stress levels would not be negatively impacted in this planting season. I trust that everything will be ordained and orchestrated by You.

Holy Spirit, remind me to take care of my temple–do not allow stress and anxiety to affect my eating, sleep, and workout habits. Do not allow the pressures of weight loss to affect my healthy health habits or mindset. I pray to carry Your confidence and I leave all worries at Your feet.

I speak "effortless" and "abundance" into this season, Lord. And I pray that You are in control of all things. I speak it and I receive that truth, in the name of Jesus.

Amen.

Scriptures

So do not fear, for I am with you; do not be dismayed, for I am your God. I will strengthen you and help you; I will uphold you with my righteous right hand.

Isaiah 41:10 (NIV)

Personal Prayers

Answered Prayers

Vision Casting With God

Wedding Be Aligned with God's Vision

Dear Lord,

You knitted our hearts to become one, I give You praise. I praise and thank You for revealing to me what true love looks and feels like. This could not have happened without You. And I thank You.

I want to include You in every single area of this marriage, Lord. Including the wedding. I know so much goes into it, but I pray that we make this totally and wholeheartedly about You and the union that You have brought together in me and __________.

Lord, You know what I desire and see as my perfect wedding. And I know that _____ may have some thoughts on it as well. I pray that we can cast a vision that would meet both of our desires for what we envision as being the perfect day.

But not only that, Lord, I pray to hear Your thoughts as well. You see our future and You know our past. You know our hearts, God. If there is anyone who would know what to include on this day to make it perfect, it would be You.

Speak to us, Lord. Your Word says that You would give us wisdom abundantly if all we do is ask for it. I'm asking for Your wisdom right now. And You also said that You would come to those who seek You. Well, Lord, I'm seeking You now.

Speak to our hearts, God. Give us visions and dreams about our wedding. About the theme, the place, the setting, and the environment. Reveal to us who should be included and who should/should not be invited. Help us to know about our reception options and which traditions to uphold.

Help us with our vows, as we prepare to make this covenant with each other and with You. Lord, if there is anything that we've planned already that You feel should not be included on our wedding day then reveal it to us now, in the name of Jesus.

Help us to honor You in every way possible. May our visions and plans honor our parents and each other. May no one get in the way to interfere with the plans that You have set in motion.

Lastly, Lord, I pray that You give _____ and I the courage and the faith to carry out the vision that You have for us. No matter how crazy or uncomfortable it may make us feel. We want to start this marriage off on the right foot, and we know that means to obey You rather than to sacrifice that opportunity to please ourselves and others.

We ask for the faith that doors will open and that You will provide in every way for the things You desire for us to have and do on our wedding day.

Amen.

Scriptures

And if it seems evil to you to serve the Lord, choose for yourselves this day whom you will serve, whether the gods which your fathers served that were on the other side of the River, or the gods of the Amorites, in whose land you dwell. But as for me and my house, we will serve the Lord.

Joshua 24:15 (NKJV)

Personal Prayers

Answered Prayers

Vision Casting With God

Wedding Traditions That Would Align With (Y)Our Values

Dear Lord,

We want to give You the total glory and credit for this marriage. And, as we prepare to become one, in front of our family and friends, I want to be sure that You are being honored during every part of our wedding day.

Lord, as we move forward in planning out the days leading up to our wedding, I ask that all of our traditions, acts, and activities will honor You. Help us to say no to things that do not hold You and our faith in the highest light. Help us to create an environment where drunkenness and debauchery are not the focus of our reception.

Give us the spirit of boldness to declare that anything our families are used to having at a wedding that displeases You will not be welcomed. Allow us to stand firm on these decisions without any major backlash from our loved ones. For as for me and our home, we shall serve You, Lord.

Lord, reveal to me any plans that are currently in motion that should be stopped. Holy Spirit, if there is anything we may be unaware of, such as our music selection, dress style of the bridesmaids' dresses or my own wedding dress, alcohol, certain dances, bachelor/bachelorette parties, and activities, or anything else we may have overlooked, I ask that you bring it to the forefront of my heart right now, in the name of Jesus.

Remind me and my fiancé that this season is all because of Your doing, Your will, and by Your blessing. Let us repay You through our actions, behaviors, and desire to honor You. No matter what.

Help me to keep that truth alive and visible. No one else should even matter–Help me to remember that if any strife or backlash comes. Let us move according to Your path. Thank You for your discernment and Your guidance.

Amen.

Scriptures

And whatever you do, in word or deed, do everything in the name of the Lord Jesus, giving thanks to God the Father through him.

Colossians 3:17 (ESV)

Personal Prayers

Answered Prayers

Vision Casting With God

Prayer for the Bridal Party

Dear Lord,

Thank You for blessing us with the family and friends we have chosen to act as our bridal party. These people have all helped bring us closer together and we are grateful for the relationship that we have with each of them.

As we prepare for this wedding and our marriage afterwards, I pray over each of the people in our bridal party. Keep them from any harm, sickness, misfortune, or anything else that would cause them stress, fear, doubt, or anxiety. Help them to remain sound and healthy in mind, body and spirit. Allow them to be blessed in their workplaces, families, home life, and anywhere else they encounter during this season.

I pray, Lord, that no one will try to overstep their boundaries during this season. Allow no bridesmaids or groomsmen to go against the plans and decisions we have made for this wedding. We brought every regard up to You, and we know that we are on the same page–please let no one try to tell us otherwise. Dismiss any thoughts or actions from the bridal party that would result in a negative impact on this wedding.

I pray right now in the name of Jesus that if there is anyone who needs to be included in this party, or if anyone should be dismissed from it, that You would make it known right now. Allow my fiancé and I to gain the wisdom and discernment needed to create a circle of loved ones within this party who will have our best interest at heart at all times.

I pray over the financial wellbeing of each of the people in my bridal party. May You provide for them all of their needs, and remove any stress they may have with regards to paying for their wedding obligations. I pray that we can be able to bless them in some way just as they are blessing us with their presence.

Lord, may everyone in our bridal party get along. Cover our friendships and relationships with Your unconditional love. Hold us accountable to Your truths and Your will for this wedding and our marriage. Help my fiancé and I to encourage, serve, and meet the needs of our bridal party as best as we can. Give us peace to work together. And give us the strength we need to serve them as they serve us.

Amen.

Scriptures

The righteous choose their friends carefully, but the way of the wicked leads them astray.

Proverbs 12:26 (NIV)

Personal Prayers

Answered Prayers

Vision Casting With God

The Wedding Day Prayer

Dear Lord,

O Lord, You are good! Marvelous are Your ways! Glorious are Your works. I delight in Your goodness and faithfulness. I bask in Your glory and all of Your splendor. Lord, today is the day that You have made and I will rejoice and be glad in it!

Lord, I am so overwhelmed with Your love and goodness today! After years of waiting and praying and trusting, You are faithful and good! Thank You, Lord, for blessing me with this day. For blessing me with a man worthy to become my husband. Thank You, Lord, for molding me into a woman who is worthy to be called "wife".

Jesus, I lift this day up to You. I pray that everything that comes from it would glorify You and You alone. I pray that every single detail of this day would be filled with Your peace and Your love. May all of the wedding preparations go smoothly. May all who are involved on my special day be healthy, happy, and reminded of your goodness.

Let there be no strife or confusion of any kind today. May all of the vendors (flowers, DJ, caterer, ______) be on time, professional, and in union with myself and my fiancé and among any family/friends who must deal with them today. I pray, Lord, that everyone involved in the wedding would be on time, including me!

I pray that there be no offense of any kind brought to or carried out on this day! I pray that those invited would honor and respect this day as being one of the most important days of my life. If they have any motives or temptations to act out, disrespect our wedding wishes, or present an attitude and/or spirit that is not pleasing to You, Lord, I pray they stay home or encounter someone who is willing to correct them in love on our behalf.

Lord, I don't wanna deal with drama, stress, or anxiety on this day. I don't want to hear about it from others. And I don't want to anticipate it for any reason. I pray, Lord, that today can be a day where I can step into my new chapter as a married woman in confidence, grace, and peace.

Lord, calm my nerves and stomach. Give me an appetite to eat and a thirst to take care of myself on this special day. Let me walk down the aisle in peace and carrying the Joy of Your Holy Spirit.

Allow me to soak up every minute of our ceremony and savor every minute of our reception. Let me remember my husband's face the moment he becomes my husband. Protect this day, Lord, and cover it with Your blessings. May a hedge of protection surround every location affiliated with this day.

Pour Your Spirit over us as we enjoy this day. I thank You, Lord, for this divine covering and for this special blessing that You have given me. Thank You.

Amen.

Scriptures

With all humility and gentleness, with patience, bearing with one another in love, eager to maintain the unity of the Spirit in the bond of peace.

Ephesians 4:2-3 (ESV)

Personal Prayers

Answered Prayers

Vision Casting With God

The Wedding Night Prayer

Dear Lord,

I've thought about this day for a very long time. But a lot of those thoughts also were regarding what's about to go down tonight.

Lord, I want this night to be special and truly unforgettable. As you say, the two become one; help me to embrace this holy union without fear, shame, or pressure.

Allow me to see my husband as Eve saw Adam for the very first time. Let there not be a sense of tension or awkwardness surrounding what I think I should know or think I should do. Instead, let it be natural. Let our love overflow any consuming thoughts I may have about spending the night with my husband as his wife.

Lord, I am most concerned about ________________. Holy Spirit, comfort me now and comfort me when those concerning moments come. I do not wish to look back on this night and think only of those concerns.

I pray no part of my impure past will be brought into my new marriage bed. I pray that the guards I have kept up all this time to protect my purity would not cause me to keep walls up against my husband.

I pray, Lord, that this experience will be good, as You have created it. Let me not focus on my past, my fears, any negative talk regarding my body image, feeling dumb or stupid for not knowing what I'm doing, not wanting to rush into this moment, perhaps not even feeling as excited as everyone tells me I should feel. Lord, I know that these are all thoughts of the enemy. I rebuke them in the name of Jesus.

At the end of the night, Lord, I want to feel love. I want to experience the true definition of what it means to "make love". I want to only focus on this day, my husband, and the unbreakable love that we have for each other. I want this night to set the rest of our nights together in a pleasing and good way.

I pray that whatever we decide to do, whether we have sex and foreplay, or simply hold each other and fall asleep in each other's arms that it would be perfect and exactly what we both need. Lord, meet us in the middle of this moment.

Your love casts out all fear–so in Your name, let there be none on this night. Our marriage and our love are honored and orchestrated by You and You alone so I trust in Your ways. I know that you will take care of my thoughts and anxiety when it comes to this special moment. I know that You will not leave us now.

I pray to have Your supernatural peace wash over me right now in the name of Jesus. And I receive this night as a wedding gift from You to us and from us to each other. I thank You, Lord, in walking me through this and for lifting away all of the pressures, doubts, insecurities, and unreal expectations that I have placed over myself all these years.

I receive Your Spirit of love and I receive Your freedom over my body in this area of my life. I embrace the beauty you have bestowed upon me since birth and I receive the natural and good sexual attraction that I have for my husband. I thank you for these blessings, gifts, and for your ever-present Holy Spirit.

Amen.

Scriptures

Therefore a man shall leave his father and his mother and hold fast to his wife, and they shall become one flesh. And the man and his wife were both naked and were not ashamed.

Genesis 2:24-25 (NKJV)

Personal Prayers

Answered Prayers

Vision Casting With God

The Honeymoon Prayer

Dear Lord,

I am so ready for this honeymoon! Just a time to relax and enjoy this new union with my husband.

Lord, wherever we have chosen to go, for however long we have decided to be gone, I pray that You would cover that time and place with Your divine protection and peace. Cover our travels, Lord, and keep us safe both coming and going.

Bless the place where we will be staying so that no evil or weapon formed against us will prosper. Protect us from scammers, robbers, or anyone who would try to take away from this experience. Protect our finances and any and all belongings we choose to bring with us.

Lord, I pray for peace throughout our entire honeymoon. I pray that we have no complications, misunderstandings, or fallouts with those whom we encounter during our honeymoon. Also, I pray that there be no strife or conflict between myself and my new husband. May this be a time of love and unity. A time for us to connect and grow to know each other as You have created and designed a husband and wife to know one another.

I pray that our love for each other reaches a new-found level of intimacy during this time. That this time together would help us set the foundation of our marriage and marriage bed for generations to come. I pray that this would be an unforgettable experience that will be carried in our hearts and actions. May the love, closeness, and faith we build together during this time be used throughout our entire marriage and serve as a living testimony that what You have brought together, no man, thing, or act can separate.

Amen.

Scriptures

My lover is mine, and I am his.

Song of Solomon 2:16 (NLT)

Personal Prayers

Answered Prayers

Vision Casting With God

Preparing For Marriage Prayers

Prayer for My Future Husband

Dear Lord,

I thank You for blessing me with my future husband. As I live and breathe, You truly are a God of Miracles. There was once a time in my life where I thought and felt that this man did not exist! And yet, You, Lord, have made a way in the wilderness and created this man especially for me. I thank You.

Lord, as I am flooded with all the details and preparations that are going into the wedding and marriage, I want to take the time now to lift up my future husband to You. He is a man worthy of a good life and a good home. I pray for his well being, sound mind, and heart.

Bring him the peace he needs to carry out what he needs to during this season. Fill him, Lord, with Your holy wisdom and discernment to guide us both towards a marriage with You at the center. Give him favor at his job and with whomever he encounters.

Speak to my future husband, Lord. Have an encounter with him. And reveal to him the ways he should go and steps he must take to set our home and future upon Your Rock. Show him what he must do now to step up as the leader of our home and marriage. Give him the strength that You possess to carry out the provisions and values our marriage must have to endure this world.

Protect him from any harm, weapons, bondage, sickness, or evil thing that tries to come his way. Help my future husband gain the sound mind that he needs to look to You and no one else. Place mentors, friends, and counselors in his life who will mold him to become more like You. Cut the ties of anyone who is deadweight for him–push him to always strive for greater.

I pray that my future husband continues to be everything that I need and want him to be. May I never fall out of love or lose my friendship with him. Help me to always address his needs when I am able to, and help him address mine. Bring us closer together, Lord. Lift up my future husband to become the man You have created him to be.

Amen.

Scriptures

He who finds a wife finds a good thing, and obtains favor from the Lord.

Proverbs 18:22 (NKJV)

Personal Prayers

Answered Prayers

Vision Casting With God

Building A Firm Marriage Foundation

Dear Lord,

I lift this marriage up to You, and everything that will come from it. I speak life and breathe faith into the union that you are creating between me and ________________.

Lord, I speak against any fears, doubts, insecurities, or weapons that may try to come against this marriage. I pray that from the very moment that we are joined together as one, that You would anoint and protect this marriage. Help us to sanctify ourselves as we learn to grow and act as one.

Remove any and all distractions, temptations, people, things, behaviors, and patterns in our lives that would lead to destruction. I ask this in Your name so that we may be able to plant a firm foundation in You.

Lord, we trust in You and we look to You for our vision and wisdom. Our help, provision, and strength come from You. You are our Rock and Strong Tower. Let not the enemy come against what You have drawn together in us.

When the storms arise, as we find ourselves in the pits and valleys, Holy Spirit, remind us of Your goodness and power. May we look to You in the good times and bad. Help us to always remember our place as Your children and rightful heirs to Your kingdom.

O Lord, I ask that strife and disunity may never come out of this marriage. May our disagreements and conflicts be short-lived and easily resolved through love and service unto one another. Make us unshakable and give us the faith we need to sustain a rock-solid friendship and relationship with each other and with You.

Amen.

Scriptures

Everyone then who hears these words of mine and does them will be like a wise man who built his house on the rock. And the rain fell, and the floods came, and the winds blew and beat on that house, but it did not fall, because it had been founded on the rock.

Matthew 7:24-25 (ESV)

Personal Prayers

Answered Prayers

Vision Casting With God

Prayer Of The Blending Of Our Families

Dear Lord,

I thank You that You are not only blessing me with a husband but with a family as well. Lord, I lift up my in-laws and the relationship that I will now have with them as their future daughter-in-law. Allow us to grow in love and accept one another as a child and their parents ought to. Show me the best way to honor them always and to always serve them out of love and respect.

I pray over my in-laws (if any) and that we can find peace and love in our interactions with one another as I grow to become a part of their family. Let us create a genuine friendship and mutual respect for one another as we tend to our own immediate families.

I pray over my new grandparents, aunts, uncles, cousins, and family friends who will now become a part of my life. May Your love and Sovereignty bring us close without any tension or conflict.

Lord, I don't want to have any offense over any of my new family members. So if there is any unsettling in my heart right now, I ask that You would reveal it to me and help me to remove it before the wedding.

If anyone has an offense over me, I pray that You would give them the strength they need to bring it up so that we can resolve it before I get married. I pray that as we prepare to leave our family to cleave to each other that You would help us to make that an easy transition.

As we begin to set up our own family values and traditions, I pray that there would be no backlash from our families or offense. May they all understand and accept in love that we are no longer individuals but a union that must create our own family dynamics. Help us in that, Lord.

If I, or my future husband, has any relationships with a particular family member that is extremely close and/or codependent, help us to leave from that as You continue to refine our cleaving process.

If I have any particularly close connections with any family members, then help me to depend more on my husband and transition out of that dependence with that family member. I know it will never replace the love that I have for them, I just wanna learn how to lean on my husband now over anyone else. Please teach me and show me how to do that.

I pray that (name of fiancé) will also have a good connection and relationship with every member of my family. May they accept him and trust him in becoming the head over our family foundation. May they fall in love with all of the qualities and attributes that I have seen and loved in him.

Lastly, Lord, if any of our family members strongly feel that we shouldn't get married, please let them come to us and speak their reservations in love. If what they are saying and feeling is true, the Holy Spirit let us have the eyes to see and the ears to hear that truth! I don't want to get defensive over something that possibly saves us from making a terrible mistake.

But, if what they are saying is not true and in alignment with Your will, allow us to reveal that and stand firm in Your plan to bring us together. Work in their hearts to submit to Your plan over us and to find peace in our decision to wed, regardless of their opinions.

While stress does come with marriage at times, I pray that none of the ongoing detrimental stress comes from our families. I lift them all up to You, Lord, from the oldest to the youngest and I pray that we would be covered by Your peace to love for all of our days.

Thank You for this gift of love in my fiancé and in our families.

Amen.

Scriptures

How good and pleasant it is when God's people live together in unity!

Psalm 133:1 (NIV)

Personal Prayers

Answered Prayers

Vision Casting With God

Submitting To My Future Husband

Dear Lord,

This is a hard prayer for me but I come to You with a sincere and truthful heart. I understand Your blueprint for a healthy family. I get the roles that You have laid out when it comes to a husband and wife. He leads, I follow.

But You raised me to be independent and strong. Surely Your way does not mean that I must choose to become anything less than. Help me, Lord, to fully understand what it means to submit to my husband and his authority. Just as Jesus submitted to the Father in the garden of Gethsemane, this is a difficult task for me to do. But I trust fully in you, Lord.

And so, I gotta trust that You are setting a leader before me who is worthy of submitting to. I gotta believe and trust that through my submission, my marriage and future will be blessed. And I'm not gonna lie, that requires a TON of faith for me! I'm asking You to give me that gift of faith, Lord.

Allow me to trust not only in You but in him so that I can serve this family as his helper and teammate. Help me to not overstep my boundaries when it comes to his leadership. May I be reminded to come to You first before acting out or being disrespectful, or trying to control the situation.

Lord, before I become a wife, I pray that You would help me in these things now. Show me how to support his leadership in our relationship now. What can I do to support him and to trust You more? Is there anything I need to stop doing now? Reveal it in my heart so that I can take care of it. So that I can open up, submit it to You so that YOU can take care of it!

Help me to see this role of submission not as a sign of weakness but as a strength that is essential to a healthy marriage and family foundation. That by submitting to my future husband, I am trusting Your plan and surrendering my control over the situations over to You. May I never forget my unique strengths and qualities that make me such a crucial part of this team.

Help me to remember that I am worth something, even if I am not the head of the home. Help me to accept my role as my future husband's helper... to accept it with an open heart and as an act of worship onto You.

Amen.

Scriptures

Wives, submit to your own husbands, as to the Lord. For the husband is the head of the wife even as Christ is the head of the church, his body, and is himself its Savior. Now as the church submits to Christ, so also wives should submit in everything to their husbands.

Ephesians 5:22 (ESV)

Personal Prayers

Answered Prayers

Vision Casting With God

Dismissing "Divorce" From My Marriage

Dear Lord,

I lift up my marriage to You as a union that will never be shaken nor broken by the enemy. I am not going all this way to have us break it off simply because things might get tough later in life!

Lord, I pray that my marriage will be protected and sustained by Your hand and Your will. I pray that the thought of divorce would never even enter our minds–even when times get tough.

Let divorce never become an option as a way of resolving our differences. I do not want to live through a marriage where divorce becomes my safety net whenever I am afraid, offended, or things go wrong. May I always look to You in times of need and as an act of desperation or consultation. Renew my mind and heart daily so that Your words are clear and Your path is the only one I see.

Help me to see what needs to be addressed now in my life and in my future husband's life so that we do not carry it into our marriage. Allow me to see the red flags that exist today so that I can address them now before it is too late.

Lord, let me walk into a marriage that is pleasing and ordained by You. If it is anything but that, I ask that You save me from moving forward right now. Allow me to see what You see, Lord, and hear what You hear. I do not wish to be the foolish bride who simply walked into a situation knowing that it was not good for me in the first place.

I do not desire to live with mistakes that would ultimately lead to a divorce. Help me, Holy Spirit, to avoid this path. Instead, I look to You for wisdom. Wisdom for now and for our future together. If it is meant to be then lead me in how I can resolve conflicts for when they arise. Also, show me how to love, serve, and submit daily so that our cord of three is not easily broken.

Thank You for sealing this marriage with Your love and Your divine security.

Amen.

Scriptures

A person standing alone can be attacked and defeated, but two can stand back-to-back and conquer. Three are even better, for a triple-braided cord is not easily broken.

Ecclesiastes 4:12 (NLT)

Personal Prayers

Answered Prayers

Vision Casting With God

Prayer Over Our Joint Finances

Dear Lord,

I've been told that a major reason why couples split is their finances. Let us not be one of those couples. Lord, I lift up our finances to You right now in the name of Jesus. May we both find the wisdom and discernment to come up with a financial plan that works for both of us and our family.

Let us be able to work through our financial differences with peace and love. Help us to see who is the saver and who is the spender. Inspire us to create financial goals early in our marriage and may Your Spirit of self-control pour out over us so that we can stick to those goals.

I speak against any financial debt or burdens we may currently have. Give us the wisdom to create a plan, make it plain, and to write it down that we should both apply it into our daily lives so that we may be able to pay them off either before we get married, or in the very early stages of our marriage. I desire to live a debt-free future so that we are not weighed down from the blessings and life that you have set for us. Once married, I pray that we do not become a family who relies heavily on credit cards, loans, and other forms of debt creation. Help us to live solely dependent on You and what You provide through our jobs and Your blessings.

Lord, give us the strength to look to You as our Provider during financial hardships. Lead us to any financial classes, programs, counselors, or any other resource that can help us to set up our financial foundation. May the foundation we set for our family rest on your Biblical principles.

Give us the heart to give to Your kingdom and to tithe diligently. May we live within our means and be able to give generously and serve as a blessing to others. Show us the best way to grow and prosper financially. Reveal to us which one should administer the finances of our home so that they are always kept in order. Give us a way out of debt so that together, we can find freedom and live in that freedom throughout our marriage.

Lord, I pray that You would cast aside any pride or selfishness when it comes to our finances. Help us both to see that our paychecks now contribute to each other and our family–that it is no longer meant only for just one or the other to spend how they please.

Help me to help my future husband in working together as a team towards financial unity, freedom, and success. Lord, I speak life over our finances in that they would be life-giving to our marriage, to others, and not life taking, robbing us of a happy, healthy marriage. I trust in You, Lord. I trust in Your provision. I trust in Your guidance, and I trust that You would meet our financial needs all of the days of our life and marriage.

Amen.

Scriptures

A good man leaves an inheritance to his children's children.

Proverbs 13:22 (NKJV)

Personal Prayers

Answered Prayers

Vision Casting With God

Prep Me For a New Season As a Wife

Dear Lord,

I cannot thank You enough for blessing me in this season of engagement. You have covered me during my singleness, and You are loving on me so much during this season. But soon, I will become a wife. And I know how easy and also difficult that can seem at times.

It seems like it will be an easy transition, considering I've wanted to be in this role for so long. But Lord, I don't want to fool myself. I'm sure there are things about this role that I have yet to consider. I pray about those things. Prepare me, Lord, to be the wife that (name of fiancé) needs.

Mold me to have the qualities and attitude that a good wife should have. Give me the fruits of Your Spirit so that I can honor my husband at all times and reflect the persona of the Proverbs 31 wife. Cause she was good! And though I may not be able to do all that she did, I want to at least create a heart in me that would reflect Your goodness.

Show me how I can put You first in my life and support my husband second. Reveal to me what I need to work on in myself that will help me prepare for this new role. Allow me to find like-minded wives whom I can relate to and seek support from whenever I need it. I know I need to trust You to make any changes in my heart and mind so that I trust You. That by the time I say "I do", I will be ready to face this new role with grace and receive this mantle with love.

I pray that I do not lose myself in this new role. Show me that You are producing a better version of myself as I move into this role. That this new identity is only a refinement of the workmanship You've already created in me. To be a wife is a blessing and an honor. Thank You for choosing me for this role.

Amen.

Scriptures

A wife of noble character is her husband's crown, but a disgraceful wife is like decay in his bones.

Proverbs 12:4 (NIV)

Personal Prayers

Answered Prayers

Vision Casting With God

Becoming One Body

Dear Lord,

As I lift up this marriage to You I want to take a moment to pray specifically about ______ and I becoming one. What a deep and profound thing that is, Lord! Like Adam and Eve, I desire to grow and nurture a marriage where we can be naked and unashamed.

Lord, strengthen our relationship, friendship, and intimacy so that no matter what comes our way, we stand and face the world together as one. One body, one heart, and one mind. As your church is instructed to be like, I pray to set our marriage and family foundation to move in one accord, acting and serving as one body that will glorify only You.

Help me, Lord, in this case, to serve and love my husband in only a way that a loving wife can serve and love her husband. Speak to me, Holy Spirit, on how and when to speak in his love language. Prompt me on when I need to love hard and when I need to respect his space.

May my love and service to him become a direct reflection of my love and worship onto You. Because yeah, even though I do this for him, ultimately, I am in this new role as a part of Your will and ultimate purpose over my life. So I want to express my gratitude in the way I steward this new role.

Lord, when _______ and I do not see eye-to-eye, remind us of the fruits of Your spirit. Pour out in me a spirit of kindness, love, peace, and self-control. Help me to bring peace into our home at all times.

May our personalities, goals, dreams, and ambitions begin to knit themselves together as one in this season so that by the time we get married, we are moving forward together.

Help us to discuss these things with each other now. Help us to speak of those disagreements now so that they may be resolved and compromised. Allow us to see the expectations we have for one another in love, service, and values. Lord, I pray that You continue to open doors that will allow us to further evolve into a body that cannot be separated by any means.

Amen.

Scriptures

And Adam said: "This is now bone of my bones and flesh of my flesh; She shall be called Woman, Because she was taken out of Man."

Genesis 2:23 (NKJV)

Personal Prayers

SELINA ALMODOVAR

Answered Prayers

Vision Casting With God

Effective Communication with My Future Husband

Dear Lord,

Thank You, Lord, for making a way for me to simply come to You anytime, anywhere, to chat and share my worries, concerns, and dreams. I love that You are always there and that I have the privilege to call upon You as my Savior, my Father, and my Friend. I pray that even in marriage, I can continue to strengthen that communication I have with you.

You have set such a wonderful example of communication for me to take into my future marriage. One that is an open-door policy. One that requires nothing in return. No shame nor judgment. I love that.

Lord, I desire to have that same kind of communication with _(name of fiancé)_. I don't ever want to feel like I have to hold anything back from him for whatever reason. Lord, let me be able to talk about anything, anytime with him. Even when I am upset and do not have the words, I pray that we would find a way to communicate even still.

Lord, let no walls or barriers linger or be built within this marriage. I pray for a marriage where we are fully engaged and comfortable going to You first and each other second for all of our needs and concerns.

May there be no secrets kept between us–except the ones that are meant to be lovely surprises to and from each other, of course. I pray that if either of us has a problem speaking our hearts or minds now, that You would reveal that so that we can begin to work to overcome that. Allow our love to expand our trust in one another so that we can communicate effectively, even before we say, "I do".

I pray we never get bored of each other's conversations, and like You, we can share a loving environment that makes it easy to approach one another, knowing that we will be loved, accepted, and never judged. Open my heart, Lord, to receive my husband and to invite him into all of my life.

Bless our communication always and teach us to use it to bless our future marriage.

Amen.

Scriptures

Let no corrupting talk come out of your mouths, but only such as is good for building up, as fits the occasion, that it may give grace to those who hear.

Ephesians 4:29 (ESV)

Personal Prayers

Answered Prayers

Vision Casting With God

Bonuses!

There is just so much that goes into your engagement season! I didn't want to just leave it all behind. So, this is the part of the book that will help you enhance the prayers you just prayed.

Here's what you can find in this section of the book:

Bonus Prayers!

While these extra prayers may not apply to every bride-to-be, I thought they would be super helpful for those who need them. These prayers deal with blended families, second marriages, and preparing for the dual role of becoming a bride and a stepmother.

Each of these prayers also come with the spaces for personal, answered, and vision casting sections.

How to Pray with your Fiancé

I'm a firm believer that you should begin praying with your Mr. Right from the very beginning of your relationship. But I also believe that when you do so, you are reaching a deeper level of intimacy, therefore you have to be careful how deep your prayers and prayer time gets at the beginning stages of your relationship.

Since you both are now engaged, it's really time to develop (or create) this intimacy so that you are prepared to take it into your marriage as husband and wife.

This bonus section will help you create that setting so that you and your fiancé can grow spiritually while staying connected to Christ as the center of your relationship.

How to Cast Vision with God

As mentioned previously, this is an important part of your planning and preparation for the next chapter of your life.

If you need assistance in making this possible in your prayer life, this section will cover some step-by-step tips you can take to cast vision over your season, wedding, and marriage.

Tips for a Smooth Engagement Season

As I mentioned before, my engagement season was truly "effortless". This was the term that Kyle and I used time and time again, simply because we felt this the most throughout our engagement experience.

So to help you gain that same experience, Kyle and I came up with a few tips that can help you and your finance! This section will dive into that.

Online Bonuses!

But wait, there's more! Be sure to go to **https://selinaalmodovar.com/ewpbresources** to receive these bonus resources that you can use during your engagement season!

- Wedding Preparation Timeline
- The Wedding Ceremony Prayer Handout (for print)
- The Wedding Reception Prayer Handout (for print)
- Wallpapers of Prayer Snippets for Your Phone
- Complete List of Books & Devotionals For Your Engagement Season

- Access to EBooks and Online Courses on Love & Relationships
- Personal Prayers, Answered Prayers, and Vision Casting with God Section Printouts

Bonus Prayers!

Prayer for My Children During My Engagement Season

Dear Lord,

Thank you for blessing me with my child(ren). They have been my heart, my life, and my whole world. I praise You for giving them to me during a time in my life when I needed to receive and give love. I don't know where I would be without them.

God, as I'm now entering into this engagement season, I want to lift up my child(ren) to You. This is not only a big change for me but it is a big change for them. As I am preparing my heart and life for a husband, they will need to also prepare their hearts and lives for a father. Help them, Lord, to prepare them for this life change.

I pray that the relationship my child(ren) have with my future husband be cultivated under Your example of love. May they grow to honor him just as they would honor me. Bring a loving relationship between them that would last a lifetime. Help my child(ren) see him as a father who loves, protects, serves, guides, and provides.

I pray that my child(ren) would feel as though they are not being left out during this time. Show them that this is something that will enhance our family unit. Help me, Lord, to include them in the celebration of our union. Reveal to me ways and moments that I can make with them so that they do not feel neglected, replaced, or abandoned.

Reveal to me any conflicts that my child(ren) may have during this season. I pray that they would find comfort in me or my fiancé to raise any issues they may have so that we can resolve them as a family. May they keep their hearts and minds open to this change and not grow bitter, resentful, rebellious, or act out of character. I pray against any fears, doubts, anxieties, disturbances, reservations, or any other issues that they have regarding this engagement and the new addition(s) to our family structure.

I pray that my fiancé would find personal ways to connect with (each of) my child(ren) so they develop a bond that is strong and formed in love. I pray that he would invest his time, talents and treasures into them. Give him a natural desire to adopt my kid(s) as his own flesh and blood. Show him how to be the father that my child(ren) need him to be. As great of a fiancé as he is to me, let me be an even greater father figure to them.

Lord, in all of this time, I have been the leader of my child(ren) in my household. But now it is time to extend that mantle to my future husband. Help me help my kid(s) to see that my fiancé is now the leader of the home. Help me to lead by example in submitting to his leadership. Show me ways that I can model this new family structure for our child(ren) moving forward so that they can learn to do it as well.

You know that my kid(s) mean everything to me, but they will one day find a spouse of their own to love and cleave onto. My husband will be the one who remains. So while I have been giving my all to my child(ren), I pray that you will help me learn to put my relationship with my future husband first, even before that of my kid(s). For the sake of Your godly family structure, help me to put him first, while also showing love and affection towards my kid(s).

Teach us, Lord, how to raise my kid(s) with dignity, integrity, love, kindness, and all of the qualities that You have blessed them with. Help us to create family memories that will be cherished for generations to come.

Amen.

Scriptures

Start children off on the way they should go, and even when they are old they will not turn from it.

Proverbs 22:6 (NIV)

Personal Prayers

Answered Prayers

Vision Casting With God

Preparing for the New Role
As a Step-Mom

Dear Lord,

To be a mother is a blessing and a gift. I am thankful and honored that I would be chosen to become such a blessing to my fiancé's child(ren). But I need Your help.

While I can never replace their biological mother, I pray God that You would help me in becoming the best mother I can be for them. Help me to be there when they need me. Show me how I can connect with them so that we can form a relationship of our own.

Help me to respect their boundaries and I pray they will respect the boundaries that I have set with their father. Show me ways that I can cultivate a loving friendship and mothering relationship with them. Reveal to me their love languages and how I can earn their trust so that we can grow close and strong.

Lord, if there is any conflict between us, I pray that You will help me find peace and resolution before the wedding. I do not want to get married knowing that the children of our family are not in total agreement.

I pray that you will open doors of opportunities for us to connect, grow, and get to know one another. Show me what it means to nurture them as a loving mother would.

Help me to find a mutual respect and love for their mother. Allow us all to agree to love and serve the child(ren) so that they can grow up in a loving and safe environment. Regardless of the relationship that their mother has with their father, I pray that I can have respect in my heart for each parent as I learn to become a parent of their child(ren).

I thank You for giving me this/these child(ren) to steward. Enlighten me with Your wisdom, patience, and love to raise them right. Help me understand what my role is in their life. Let them see me as a blessing and a good thing. Soften their heart(s) towards me so that they learn to trust and respect me. May they see me as their mother and not as a bad person.

I pray for this (these) child(ren) who will soon become my own. I pray to feel the love for them that I would feel for any one of my own. You are bringing us together to form a new family–protect us from the enemy and whatever he may try to throw at us. Keep us from any negative thoughts, reactions, or judgments that would pull us apart rather than bring us together.

Just as I am trusting my wedding and marriage to you, I also lift up this (these) child(ren) and pray over them and our future family household. Bless us in all ways and in all seasons.

Amen.

Scriptures

Don't you see that children are God's best gift? The fruit of the womb his generous legacy? Like a warrior's fistful of arrows are the children of a vigorous youth. Oh, how blessed are you parents, with your quivers full of children! Your enemies don't stand a chance against you; you'll sweep them right off your doorstep.

Psalm 127:3-5 (MSG)

Personal Prayers

Answered Prayers

Vision Casting With God

Prayer For My Second (or Third) Marriage

Dear Lord,

I am coming to You in total trust. I surrender this relationship to You and anything else that comes from it hereafter. While my previous marriage(s) did not work out, I know that You have restoration in my future. I ask to receive that completely as I move towards this new marriage.

Lord, I value Your Word. I trust in Your truth and promises. And I want to do this right. If it is not of Your will that I should be married again, or married with this particular person, then reveal it to me at once. I surrender my desires and my dreams to You and Yours.

If this door remains open, and it is indeed Your will that I wed this man, then I pray for a total restoration. I pray that whatever the enemy has stolen from me in my previous marriage, that You would restore it back to me tenfold. May this be a completely new beginning where You are at the very center of it all!

God, help me to dismiss my baggage from my previous marriage(s). My fiancé is not my ex-husband. Please help me not to treat him like he is. Help me tear down the walls that I have built in trying to protect myself and my heart from what happened to me in the past. Help me to leave the past in the past and not look back. Make this new grounds, new territory, and new love.

Lord, I am not the same woman that I used to be. I pray that every day of this season and in my future marriage, You will help me to grow to become a better version of myself. Help me to be the wife that my fiancé needs me to be and not the wife I used to be before. Keep me close to You and Your ways. Show me daily what I can do to grow and evolve into a woman and wife of God.

May I never forget the lessons that You have taught me during my first marriage. But may I also never forget the deliverance, grace, and mercy You showed me as that first marriage ended. For that reason, I want to include You in every single aspect of this relationship moving forward.

You have given me a second chance at love! And I am thankful and grateful for that. Help me to do it right this time around. Show me how I can learn to love better, serve better, communicate better, and invest in my marriage. Help me to respect my future husband and submit to him the way a godly wife should.

May I never think about ending this marriage that You have created. Let Your will be done in this marriage and in my life forever.

Amen.

Scriptures

And to put on the new self, created after the likeness of God in true righteousness and holiness.

Ephesians 4:24 (ESV)

Personal Prayers

Answered Prayers

Vision Casting With God

If The Engagement Breaks Off

Dear Lord,

I don't even know what to say. I'm confused and hurt and sad. I am deeply affected by this decision. Whether this was a decision of my own or that of my fiancé, I gotta believe that it was ultimately a decision of Yours. Help me to believe that all things happen for Your glory.

Right now, I am very much in need of love and guidance. Help me to feel and receive Your love. Reassure me and bring me confirmation that this was the right thing to do. I want to be obedient in Your will and I need to know that this was of Your will.

Give me peace, Lord. The kind that surpasses all understanding. Because right now, I'm not quite sure I understand what just happened. How could the relationship get this far only to end? Was it because I didn't hear Your direction before? Was it because something occurred that caused You to close the door?

I know that I am only but a vapor in the wind. I know that You don't ever have to answer to me. And I need to be ok with that. Help my heart trust in You to the point where I'm ok, even if I never receive the answers for these questions.

At the end of the day, I trust in You.

I know that You have something good for me. That I am worth a love that reflects Your goodness. And that I deserve to be happily married with a man whom You have created to be my husband.

I stand on this truth, God, and I rest on Your promises. I lean into Your strength during this time and I am confident that sooner or later, I will feel ok about this decision.

Protect me from making any poor choices during this time. Surround me with people who will support me and encourage me to look to You whenever I feel down or upset. Give me the reassurance I need to continue to keep and grow my faith as a new season of my life begins.

Open the doors that are meant to be opened. I seek Your Counsel, God, during this time; wisdom and discernment for what I must now do and who I must now surround myself with. Heal my heart, Lord, from any hurt that I'm feeling at this moment.

Peace, God. That's what I need right now. I'm trusting in You.

Amen.

Scriptures

Trust in the LORD with all your heart and lean not on your own understanding; in all your ways submit to him, and he will make your paths straight.

Proverbs 3:5-6 (NIV)

Personal Prayers

Answered Prayers

Vision Casting With God

How To Pray With Your Fiance

Praying with your fiancé is going to be a gradual process. Because prayer is an intimate thing that you do with God, it will take some time to blend your prayer lives together. Don't rush it. But consistency is key. The more you both pray together, the easier it will get to pray together.

To start, you can join in simple prayers. Pray when you first see each other and before you leave. Pray in church and group settings. Pray over your food. The normal stuff.

After a while, if and when you feel comfortable, begin to pray over your wedding and engagement season together. Lift up more serious prayers that your heart is open to praying about with him.

Once you are both able to pray out loud together on deeper issues, try to set up some time where you are both able to worship together. Spend quality time in worship. Sit still in God's presence. Do what feels right to you.

Remember, this is going to be a gradual process. You cannot expect to get deep and intimate in prayer with your fiancé simply because you are now engaged. You may have two totally different worship styles. And your prayer life may be completely different. Let's not forget to mention that your hearts are different, so what you spend time praying about will also differ.

You have to be open to accepting the worship and prayer style that your fiancé has, and vice versa. There is no one right way to do this. It's a heart condition. If you both are heartfelt and genuinely connecting to God during this time, then that's all that matters.

It's important to also note that in the Godly structure for marriage, the husband is the leader of the home (Ephesians 5:23). Because of this, you have to allow your future husband to lead in this time. What I mean by this is that you cannot force this spiritual connection to happen–allow your fiancé to make it so. Let him lead in heading up these moments with God. Allow him to lead in prayer. And encourage him to take the lead!

Whether or not you are more of a prayer/worshipper than he is, allow him to find his role in your future marriage by taking the lead in bringing you both spiritually closer. It may require some getting used to, but it will ultimately help him take his role as the leader of your marriage more seriously. And don't worry, God will prepare him for that role just as He will prepare you for yours. Trust in God to help you through this process. As long as you both are remaining close to Him, He will bring you both closer together as a result.

Joint Prayer List

Joint Answered Prayers

Notes from Joint Prayer Time with Your Fiancé

How To Cast Vision with God

1) **Set a time where you (and your Fiancé) can come together with God.** This can and should be an ongoing time throughout your engagement season. The more you seek God, the more you'll connect and hear from Him.

2) **Through prayer, bring your petitions to Him.** Any visions, desires, ideas, or dreams that you may have regarding your wedding, your honeymoon, and your future marriage (new home, new setup, etc.) should be spoken openly and honestly during your prayer time.

3) **As you lift your prayers up to God, patiently wait to hear back.** Keep the "Vision Casting with God" section open and be ready to jot down anything you hear during this time of

prayer. It may not be a literal sense of hearing, but you may feel something from your heart, or see something in your mind. Whatever comes up, simply jot it down.

4) **Recognize any and all visions that you (and your Fiancé) receive.** You might be reminded of scriptures, people to connect with, particular venues, or other such things. Or, you could either feel the peace to move forward in a decision or the uneasiness of a closed door. Whatever you feel, have faith that you are feeling, hearing, and seeing these visions come from God.

5) **Seek confirmation of the visions you casted.** Confirmation can come in various ways. Someone can mention it as a Word of encouragement and it matches exactly what you revealed during your time of prayer. You can read it in Scripture or a devotional and it aligns with what you felt. Or you can simply hear your vision again in some other means. No matter how the confirmation comes, it will always be aligned with God's truth and love. So, if you receive something that feels stressful, uneasy, or not peaceful, then that's not a confirmation to the vision you casted with God!

Tips for a Smooth Engagement Season

1) **Take your time.** Yes, it's possible for you to plan and have a wedding in less than a year, but if you can, slow things down a bit. Try to plan your wedding at least a year out. The reason we say this is because you won't stress as much over the longer period of time. You'll have more vendors to choose from, especially since most of them are usually booked a year out in advance! Also, you'll be able to space out your planning so that you don't feel like everything has to be done at once! Spacing out your engagement for at least a year will allow you to set up the rest of your years together with time

to plan thoroughly while also enjoying the season.

2) **Plan dates where wedding talk is prohibited or minimal at the very least.** Believe me, this event can and will consume you! This is why you have to take a Sabbath, if you will, by going on dates and getting back to you as a couple! Remember, the wedding is just a day, your marriage is a lifetime. So make the time to enjoy each other! Remind yourselves of why you're getting married in the first place. There is so much more to enjoy and talk about than this one event that is ultimately going to come and go! Make memories with each other in this season so that you can look back one day and cherish them.

3) **Focus on premarital counseling.** This is so good for you! The reason why is because it will help you discuss things that you wouldn't normally think to talk about. It can smooth out any issues or concerns you might have before saying, "I do". During your premarital counseling, you can learn the roles of a husband and wife, understand the family structure as designed by God, and learn about the expectations that you both have for each other once you become married. You can also get on the same page when it comes to traditions, values, finances, house rules, boundaries, sex

and romance, kids, pets, goals, and so much more! Ask your pastor or church where you plan to have your wedding about premarital counseling services. For a list of resources and books you can use to help you in your premarital counseling sessions, go to the bonus resource page at:

https://selinaalmodovar.com/EWPBResources

4) **Invest the first half of your season to premarital counseling, and then leave the second half for executing your wedding/ house planning.** This helped us a lot! Especially since most of the decisions and party planning projects (e.g. invitations, party favors, decorations, etc.) don't have to be done until closer to the wedding date. By focusing first on your marriage with premarital counseling, you'll have a better understanding of how to communicate with your fiancé and what each of you desire in your future. With that knowledge at hand, it'll be much easier to accomplish everything else! For anyone who tells you that you don't need to do this until closer to the wedding, simply start a premarital study on your own:

5) **Delegate wedding tasks to more than just the bridal party.** This is often how a Bridezilla becomes a Bridezilla, and also how a lot of unnecessary stress is created. Everyone has an opinion of what's best. Everyone wants to feel like they know the most. But in reality, they just want to feel included. So for any parents, grandparents, aunts, or big sisters who are trying to "steal the show" with their expertise or opinions, simply give them something to be in charge of! This will not only take their minds off of everything else, but it will also engage them in such a way that they feel honored to have been a part of your special day. For example, my mother-in-law helped with our invitations and my mother accompanied me to my dress fittings. My grandmother contributed her recipes for the food, while my husband's grandma helped us with our centerpieces. Everyone had a role to play and that helped us balance our to-do list.

Now What?

Amen! You made it to the end of this book! I hope that these prayers have given you a new faith and spiritual growth you need for this particular season of your life.

Now that you've completed this book, you might be asking yourself, "What now?" Here are several options you have:

1. **Read it again.** Because the Word tells us to never cease our prayers, you can start again on page one and pray over your engagement season all over again! And, if you completed each personal prayer section, then you'll experience a totally new and different prayer and devotional time, allowing you to go deeper into your prayers with God. Not to mention, you

can add any answered prayers you may have had along the way.

2. **Pass it along.** We all know the saying, "Something old, something new, something borrowed, something blue", well, how amazing would it be if you passed this book down to someone who can call this their "old", "borrowed", or "blue" (yes, the cover of this book is blue!)? Let's start a bridal movement! There are women in your circle who may be going through something that this book can help them with. If you had an awesome time reading this book, and praying these prayers, then care and share!
3. **Tell the world.** If this book was a total game changer for you and you just have to share it with someone (anyone!), then tell why not tell the world! Write a review on the site where you purchased this book (Or, you can share on places like Goodreads, Amazon, or my website, SelinaAlmodovar.com!) You can even post a pic with it and share online using the hashtag, #engagedwomansprayerbook (don't forget to mention me, @SelinaAlmodovar so I can see it and repost!) Your reviews and social media posts will definitely help inspire the next bride-to-be to make the decision (as you once did) to get this book and start praying for their own season of engagement!

Notes

Notes

Notes

Acknowledgments

If I ever won an award where I had twenty seconds to give thanks, I would be scared out of my mind that I would forget some of the most amazing people!

Luckily, I had some time with this and so I think I was able to cover most. Though, if I happen to forget some, my apologies. It certainly takes a village to raise a woman of God, an entire world when that woman is writing a book about Him.

First and foremost, I give thanks to God. For Your grace in my life and for restoring me from the inside out! It was because of Your hope, strength, wisdom, peace, and patience in me that I was able to set my path aligned with Your will and move forward. Your love has redefined my life and all that it encompasses. You gave me a new life and an eternal life—I pray that my gifts and these books are pleasing and good to You for Your glory.

To my amazing husband, Kyle. Where would I even be without you? You have supported me and my dreams since day one and I cannot express how much that has helped me believe in myself. You truly are God's perfect gift to me. I cherish our friendship, our love, and our future together.

To my beautiful boys, William and Solomon. While you may not know it yet, you have been such a driving force in my life. It is because of you that I press on and I do not quit. I am honored to be your mother and to have the privilege to love you and to pray over you always. While I cannot serve and protect you for all of your life, you better believe that I promise to do so for all of mine.

To my mothers, Mom (Maria) and Nancy, thank you! Thank you for always believing in my talent to write and to make something out of that writing. Thank you for always supporting me and doing whatever you can to share my joys with the world.

To Becky, one of the last things you did before joining God in heaven was purchase my book to share with someone else. I will never, ever forget your support and faith in me. I promise to continue making you proud.

To Madrina, Anita. You were such an important person during my engagement season. You taught us how to keep Christ at the very center. And your prayers are felt even to this very day. I appreciate EVERYTHING you have done for me, my marriage, and my family.

To Pastor Bob and Yolanda Kistemaker, I thank you for pastoring such an amazing church and for being obedient to the Word of God. Without you, I would have never met my husband! And together, we would have never known how to draw near to God and to allow Him to lead in our marriage.

Thank you.

To Angela, Sissy, Luz, Phyllis, and Michele, you ladies paved the way for me of what a true prayer warrior looks like. Before you came into my life, I wouldn't dare utter a prayer out loud. And because you have entered my life, I have seen what powerful prayers can do. Thank you for taking me under your wings and for guiding me into the prayer woman that I am today.

To my amazing friends, Ellen, Tasia, Amanda, Katie, and Laura. You were my support team the entire time I was writing this book. Even after taking a complete year off to focus on motherhood, you all were there to lift me up, make me laugh, and keep me going. I am blessed to have friends like you. I would have never finished this book had it not been for you.

To Katie (again) for your beautiful book cover design. And for just jumping right in when I needed you, anytime for any reason. I love you and your servant heart. Thank you for making this beautifully possible.

To Dallas Hodge, my editor and book formatter, thank you for your diligent work and for your positive service through and through! You made a way for my dreams to come true. You truly are God send!

To Enid and the Imperishable Beauty Team, I thank you for your ongoing support in my writing and with this book. Your faith in me causes me to stretch out further than I ever thought I could. Thank you for being in my corner always.

To my beautiful, amazing, truly amazing, fans, followers, and subscribers. You are my tribe! You are the reason I do this. You are my answered prayers. I am thankful and grateful that you have found hope, love, and faith from my works. Together, we will grow in faith and continue to give glory to God for all He has done, and will do in our lives! This is for you.

ALSO AVAILABLE FROM

Selina Almodovar

Just when she hit her lowest breakup point, Selina Almodovar decided to do something that would change the way she loved forever: she prayed.

Now, Selina shares her personal prayers that lead her to a deep and meaningful relationship with Jesus, healing, and love for herself, confidence and contentment during her season of singleness, and you guessed it: a loving marriage with her Mr. Right!

AVAILABLE AT: SELINAALMODOVAR.COM

Selina Almodovar

Continue feeling encouraged to trust God with your love-life...

selinaalmodovar.com

 SelinaAlmodovar-love

 @SelinaAlmodovar

 @SelinaAlmodovar

 @SelinaAlmodovar

 Selina Almodovar

 Selina@SelinaAlmodovar.com

Made in the USA
Middletown, DE
07 April 2022

63812761R00146